A PTERODACTYL
the story of a flying reptile

BEVERLY HALSTEAD

(Reader in Geology and Zoology, Reading University)

pictures by
JENNY HALSTEAD

COLLINS

William Collins Sons & Co Ltd
London · Glasgow · Sydney · Auckland
Toronto · Johannesburg

First published 1985
© text Beverly Halstead 1985
© illustrations Jenny Halstead 1985

British Library Cataloguing in Publication Data

Halstead, L.B.
A Pterodactyl: the story of a flying reptile.
1. Pterodactyls—Juvenile literature
I. Title
567.9'7   QE862.07
ISBN 0-00-104124-X

Photograph of fossilized pterodactyl the property of
Freunde der Bayerischen Staatssammlung für Paläontologie
und historische Geologie München.
Made and printed in Hong Kong
by South China Printing Co.

For Abbie

Introduction

One hundred and fifty million years ago during the Upper Jurassic period in what is now southern Germany, the body of a small pterosaur or flying reptile was washed up on the shore of a tropical lagoon. In 1784 an Italian, C. A. Collini, described this first complete skeleton, believing it to be a swimming creature. It was not until 1809, that the Frenchman Baron Georges Cuvier proved that the skeleton was that of a winged reptile to which he gave the name *Pterodactylus* or 'wing finger', because each wing was supported on a single, extended fourth finger, the first three forming a small clawed hand. Footprints show that the first toe was short, the other four long and slender. Later he suggested a second name *longirostris* because of its long snout or rostrum. In 1970 the Russian scientist G. Sharov discovered a pterosaur, *Sordes pilosus* which had the coarse hairy covering actually preserved. The pterodactyl had large eyes and a well developed brain which indicates good eyesight and sense of balance and was an efficient and highly manoeuvrable flier. The nostrils were just in front of the eyes about halfway down the snout. Its bones were light and hollow exactly like those of birds.

For 140 million years throughout the age of dinosaurs, pterosaurs dominated the skies all over the world. The largest, the vulture-like *Quetzelcoatlus* had a wing-span of 10m. In this story we shall follow the life history of a small *Pterodactylus longirostris*, which had a wing-span of 300mm, and whom we have called Rostri.

A mother pterodactyl was sitting on her eggs in the pebbles and sand among the leaves of the undergrowth, when she felt a movement under her. Her four eggs were beginning to crack. One by one four bedraggled chicks emerged. Within minutes, their coats dried and they wobbled in the nest as mottled balls of fluff. The largest was Rostri. The mother carefully picked out the broken eggshells with her long-toothed beak and dropped them well away from the nest, so that they would not attract enemies to her newly-hatched young.

The mother nestled down and the chicks snuggled into the warm furry covering under her leathery wings. At intervals she flew off and came back with a beakful of juicy insects.

The early stages of the pterodactyl's life history are based on those of birds that lay their eggs on exposed nests on or near the ground. The down-covered chicks hatch with their eyes open and are able to run about almost immediately. Although able to forage for their own food the chicks usually stay near the nest as they need extra food brought by their parents, who catch insects on the wing. Although no undisputable pterodactyl eggs have been found, it can be assumed that pterodactyls laid eggs, as all their relatives were egg-laying creatures.

After a few days the chicks left the nest and went foraging for spiders and beetles in the undergrowth. All around them crickets chirped and jumped out of their way. Rostri was about to snap up a juicy insect when he was startled by the sudden appearance of four large round eyes. Confused, he jumped backwards, fluttering his wings, and at that moment the butterfly-like insect flapped its wings and flew off.

The fossil lacewing *Kalligramma*, which resembles a butterfly, has large eyespots preserved on its wings. It is the presence of four eyespots suggesting two enemies rather than one that creates the startling effect. Also found in the same rocks are crickets, beetles, lacewings and cicadas. The special organs on crickets' wings which make the sounds are also preserved as fossils.

One day Rostri heard heavy footsteps approaching and a tearing sound as the plants round about were ripped up. The chicks fluttered off in all directions as the brontosaur *Dicraeosaurus* munched its way through the undergrowth. As it passed, insects flew up into the air and were quickly snapped up by the chicks.

The 13m long brontosaur *Dicraeosaurus*, half the length of *Apatosaurus* or *Brontosaurus*, was discovered in East Africa with remains of pterosaurs in rocks of the same age. There was no grass at this time but there were many ferns, clubmosses and horsetails; there were stumpy cycads with radiating fronds and conifer trees. Abundant fossil remains of the Gingko or maidenhair tree are found throughout Europe, North America and Asia in rocks of Jurassic age.

At three weeks, by energetically flapping their leathery wings, the young pterodactyls were able to keep themselves in the air just above the ground. Soon they were following their parents higher up into the air. Attracted by the commotion, the flesh-eaters *Compsognathus* ran out of the undergrowth. One leapt up and caught a chick with its clawed hands. Its wing torn, the young pterosaur was dragged away, squawking, to be eaten. Rostri and the surviving chicks fluttered hastily away to hide among the foliage.

The small flesh-eater *Compsognathus* has been found with the remains of the longtailed gekko *Bavarisaurus* preserved in its stomach. It would have been able to catch pterodactyl chicks easily, grabbing them with its long, clawed, two-fingered hands.

When the chicks could fly they roosted high in the trees, hanging upside down with their wings wrapped round their bodies. Sometimes a gekko or skink would run up the trunk and along the branches hunting insects. One day the feathered *Archaeopteryx* climbed the tree and surprised the pterodactyls by snatching a dozing young one in the claws on its wing.

We know that pterodactyls roosted like bats because their four long toes could only hook over the branches; they were incapable of perching which needs at least one toe facing in the opposite direction. Five specimens of **Archaeopteryx**, the first true bird, have been found in the same rocks as the pterodactyls. As well as feathers, it had teeth, a long bony tail and three claws on each wing. The bright blue colouring is based on a carnivorous tropical bird, the male vanga shrike. Lizards, the slow-worm **Dorsetisaurus**, the skink and gekko have also been found in rocks of the Upper Jurassic period.

In order to leave the branch, Rostri opened his wings, let go his grip and glided slowly through the air for a short distance. As soon as he was away from the tree he started to flap his wings. Once, when Rostri and the other pterodactyls had just left the roost, a long-tailed pterosaur *Rhamphorhynchus*, with large teeth, dived down out of the sky and, just missing Rostri, caught one of his brothers in its sharp beak.

> The long-tailed and toothed ***Rhamphorhynchus*** fed mainly on fish which it caught by diving out of the sky onto them. A slowly gliding pterodactyl would have been an easy target.

Rostri joined a flock of pterodactyls that were following small plant-eating dinosaurs, the chicken-sized fabrosaurs, as they foraged for tender plants. Where the ground was more marshy Rostri caught larger insects on the wing such as dragonflies, damselflies and scorpionflies. Then he spotted a large *Stegosaurus* plodding past, eating as it went. Rostri and other pterodactyls quickly flew onto its back. In this way they had a good supply of insects which flew up out of the plants disturbed by the *Stegosaurus*.

> Small herbivorous fabrosaur dinosaurs of the same age as the pterodactyls were discovered in 1984 in North America. We know that *Stegosaurus* the plated dinosaur, which lived at this same time, was a plant-eater from its teeth and jaws.

As they rode along, distant rumblings could be heard, there were enormous explosions and huge clouds of smoke rose into the sky from the mountains to the north. Rostri and the other pterodactyls flew off in fright, heading away from the explosions. Soon a hot cloud rolled over the area, engulfing the trees which burst into flames. The stegosaur and other slow moving dinosaurs could not escape and were soon killed by breathing the hot poisonous gases.

There are two main types of volcano: those that are explosive and throw out clouds of gases and ash and others out of which streams of lava flow. It was the explosive kinds that were active in Europe at the time of the pterodactyls.

In what is now the North Sea, 150 million years ago, the Earth's crust cracked, volcanoes erupted and clouds of hot ash fell over large distances. These ashes changed into special minerals now found in rocks. It is these minerals which prove the existence of volcanic activity.

Rostri and the flock flew over a wide flat landscape and reached a narrow expanse of sea. They landed near the coast, in an area of quiet lagoons, along the shores of creamy white muds. Small crabs, lobsters and shrimps, trapped in the mud as the tide went out, were picked up by Rostri's long beak. Along the strandline there were plenty of insects, as well as sea slaters, on which the pterodactyls feasted. A giant flesh-eater *Megalosaurus,* that had recently eaten an enormous meal, was resting with its mouth open, dozing peacefully in the sun. The pterodactyls flew around picking out bits of meat stuck between his teeth.

The limestone rock from southern Germany contains the remains of many different kinds of lobsters, crabs and shrimps, even a mantis shrimp, as well as sea slaters (relatives of woodlice). In some instances their remains can be seen at the end of the trackways made as they crawled through the muds just before they died. Tooth picking and the removal of parasites from the mouths of carnivorous animals by birds is well known.

As the tide came up the lagoon, Rostri and the other pterodactyls sat on log-like objects floating in the water, waiting for shoals of small fish to wash in with the tide. It was a nasty moment when a "log" suddenly opened its mouth to snap at the pterodactyls.

Rostri flew off squawking and stood on top of a stumpy cycad, flapping his wings and showing off his newly-acquired plume of filaments on his head. Soon a female from the flock came and joined him. They mated and after scooping a shallow nest in the sandy soil in the undergrowth, she laid her first clutch of five eggs.

In the same rocks as pterodactyls shoals of small fish, *Leptolepis sprattiformis* ("sprats") have also been found.

Some fossil pterodactyls have plumes preserved and these were probably display features. They may have been brightly coloured. As with many modern tropical animals, there is likely to have been a specific breeding season in the spring.

While Rostri was incubating the eggs a small herd of the plant-eating dinosaurs *Camptosaurus* browsing on the plant undergrowth came crashing through the nesting site and Rostri and the other pterodactyls flew up into the air for safety. As the herd passed, their large hoofed feet crushed many of the nests underfoot. All Rostri's eggs were smashed.

Rostri and his mate found another nest site, between the roots of a large tree, and there a new clutch was laid, which this time safely hatched.

Camptosaurus was about 5m long and lived in herds as shown by the evidence of footprints. Although they generally walked on their hind legs, hoofprints of the front feet show that when feeding or walking slowly they went on all fours.

In a clearing behind the lagoon, Rostri spotted the corpse of a plant-eating dinosaur being torn apart by several young flesh-eating *Ceratosaurus*. Small *Coelurus* darted in and out, snatching morsels of food, and clouds of insects swarmed over the rotting flesh. Rostri and other pterodactyls feasted off the swarms of insects and loose pieces of meat.

We can assume that flesh-eaters scavenged dinosaur corpses as bones have been found carrying scratches which match teeth marks. Broken teeth have also been found nearby.

One afternoon the sky darkened, there were flashes of lightning in the black clouds, a strong wind began to blow. The air suddenly went cold and large hailstones the size of pebbles, crashed down. As the storm broke, three of Rostri's chicks were killed outright by the giant hailstones smashing into them, but the other two miraculously escaped. Most of the adults survived as they were hanging onto the branches of the trees and were protected from the direct impact of the hailstones.

Then the main force of the storm struck. The fierce wind and torrential rain tore the branches from the trees, hurling the pterodactyls into the sky.

Prints are preserved in sandstone rocks which prove the existence of fierce storms.

As the storm raged the pterodactyls were blown hither and thither like dead leaves. The flock was swept out to sea and when the storm had blown itself out the pterodactyls were far from land and exhausted. They did not have the strength to fight their way back and fell wearily into the sea where they floated on the surface for a short while, but soon their fur became waterlogged.

When the grey dawn broke, the wind dropped and a cool breeze blew towards the shore. Rostri's body and others from the flock washed up onto the beach and were quickly covered by fine limy muds.

A perfect fossil skeleton was discovered 150 million years later in 1784, the jaws were open, the head bent back over the body, the wings swept backwards and the legs spreadeagled.